Ding Dolly

Written and illustrated by
An Vrombaut

Collins

Max is in his bat box.

3

It is Jill.

Max lets her in.

Jill has a big ring.

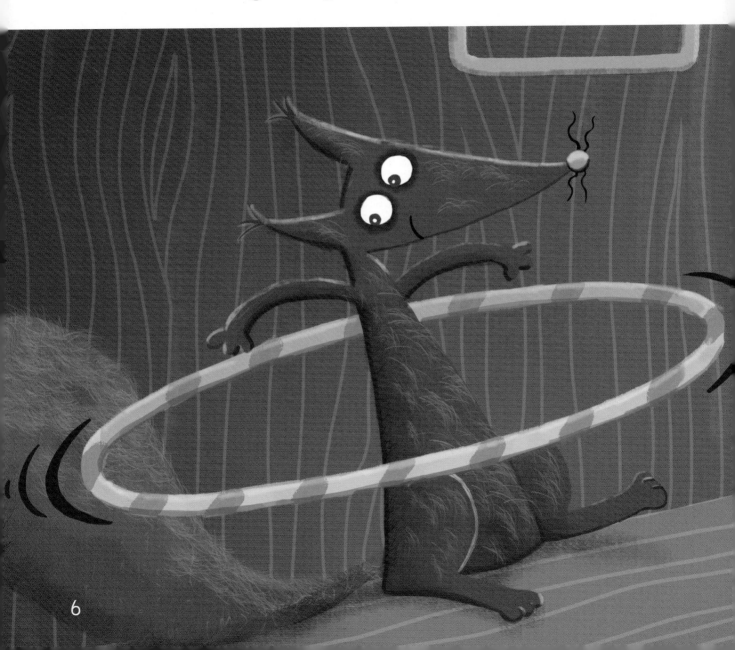

Ding dong!

It is Jack.

He has dolls.

The bat box is full.

Max rings.

Ding dong! Ding dong!

🐾 Review: After reading 🐾

Use your assessment from hearing the children read to choose any GPCs, words or tricky words that need additional practice.

Read 1: Decoding

- Ask the children to sound talk and blend each of the following words: d/i/ng, s/i/ng, r/i/ng and w/i/ng.
- Ask the children:
  - Which of the following words contain the /ng/ sound?
    Jack   sing   ping   fox   box   long   (*sing, ping, long*)
- Look at the "I spy sounds" pages (14–15) together. Discuss the picture with the children. Can the children see any pictures of things that contain the /j/ and /x/ sounds? (*jam, jelly, juice, jug, Jack-in-a-box, jeep, taxi, fox, x-ray, Max*)

Read 2: Prosody

- Model reading each page with expression to the children. After you have read each page, ask the children to have a go at reading with expression.
- On pages 3, 7 and 13, show the children how you read the words **ding dong** with expression as if a bell were ringing and encourage children to use different voices and tones.

Read 3: Comprehension

- For every question ask the children how they know the answer. Ask:
  - Why do you think the story was called "Ding Dong"? (*because it is about the bell ringing, it describes the noise a bell makes*)
  - Who comes to visit Max? (*Jill the squirrel and Jack the bird*)
  - Jill and Jack both take toys to the bat box. What is your favourite toy and why?
  - Why do you think Max rings the bell on pages 12 and 13? (e.g. *It is time for his friends to go home*)